WISDOM IN CHINESE PROVERBS

增广贤文

Written by
Chen Wangheng & Li Xiaoxiang

Translated by
Gong Lizeng & Yang Aiwen

⚜ ASIAPAC • SINGAPORE

Publisher
ASIAPAC BOOKS PTE LTD
996 Bendemeer Road #06-08/09
Singapore 339944
Tel: (65) 6392 8455
Fax: (65) 6392 6455
Email: asiapacbooks@pacific.net.sg

Come visit us at our Internet home page
www.asiapacbooks.com

First published August 1996
6th edition April 2005

Cover illustration by Xu Liyan & Poh Yih Chwen
Cover design by Chin Boon Leng
Body text in 8/9 pt Helvetica
Printed in Singapore by Chung Printing

Publisher's Note

Asiapac Books is proud to bring you this new comics on *Wisdom In Chinese Proverbs*. This book contains a collection of ancient aphorisms selected from a book called *Zengguang Xianwen* which was written nearly a thousand years ago.

Zengguang Xianwen was written in classical Chinese and includes certain philosophical theories of life that may be hard to understand. Therefore, in reproducing the stories in comics, we hope that it will appeal to the masses, especially the younger generation, and help promote the quintessence of the Chinese culture.

To reinforce your understanding and application of the proverbs, we have included matching exercises based on some common proverbs after the comics section.

We would like to express our gratitude to Professors Chen Wangheng and Li Xiaoxiang for their compilation, and to Gong Lizeng and Yang Aiwen for their translation. Our thanks, too, to Xu Liyan for her conceptualization and Poh Yih Chwen for her finished artwork and lively illustrations. Our appreciation also goes to the production team for putting in their best effort in the publication of this book.

About the Authors

Prof Chen Wangheng, born in 1944, is a scholar, writer and academic. Currently, he is with the Philosophy Department of Wuhan University in Hubei Province.

A prolific writer, he has published many works, including: *On Beauty in the Realm of Art and Literature*, *Artistic Beauty*, *Mystery of Artistic Creation*, *A Probe into the Realm of Aesthetics*, *Hegel's Treatises on Aesthetics*, *Ferocious Beauty*, *Spiritual Conflict and Harmony*, *Principles of Scientific and Technical Aesthetic Judgement*, *Principles of Scientific and Technical Aesthetics*, *Divination Practice and Philosophical Theories*, *Landscape Beauty and Psychology*, and *The Dragon Soars and the Phoenix Flies*.

Prof Li Xiaoxiang, born in 1946, is currently the Deputy Editor-in-Chief of the Wuhuan University Press.

Upon her graduation from Hunan Teachers' University, she has taught Chinese Language at pre-university level as well as worked in the Economic Department of the Zhejiang University's Higher Education Research Centre.

She has a deep understanding of Chinese language and literature. In particular, she is well-versed in Buddhism.

About the Translators

Gong Lizeng and Yang Aiwen are senior translators at the Morning Glory Publishers in Beijing, China. They have been doing translation work for years, especially the translation of books on Chinese culture, art and history. Their translated works include *Chinese Eunuchs*, *Wu Zetian*, *Wisdom in Chinese Proverbs*, and *Best Chinese Myths* published by Asiapac Books.

Introduction

Wisdom In Chinese Proverbs is a collection of comic strips designed to illustrate wise and witty sayings of ancient China. The themes of the comics were selected from a book called *Zengguang Xianwen* 增 廣 賢 文 which is an enlarged anthology of ancient aphorisms compiled sometime between the Northern Song and Yuan Dynasties, nearly a thousand years ago. It appeared at about the same time as the *Sanzi Jing* 三字 經 (*Three-Word Scripture*) and *Baijia Xing* 百家 姓 (*Hundred Chinese Surnames*) and was widely read in those days, though no one as yet knows who the author was.

Zengguang Xianwen was written in a free and easy style that dispensed with the traditional rules of matching tones and rhythm. It contains a rich collection of proverbs, idioms, maxims, legends, anecdotes, historical facts and well-turned phrases, both to help readers acquire cultural knowledge and to acquaint them with certain truths and principles of life. Among other things, it teaches people to work hard and aim high, to be honest with others and mindful of one's own conduct and behaviour, to respect the elderly and love one's parents, to be practical and realistic, to be tactful and ready to help others, to promote the good and shun the evil, to foster good friendships and detest evildoers.

Although the important principles mentioned above on how to conduct oneself and deal with others were formulated centuries ago, they are by no means out of date. On the contrary, they will help the present generation to truly understand the traditional virtues and cultural values cherished by people in the East. Many of the wise and famous sayings may be aptly described as ' terse but comprehensive, every word a pearl' . A few examples are: ' One who does not burn incense at ordinary times will have to embrace the Buddha's feet and pray for help in times of emergency' ; ' Money is a mere mass of muck; kindness is worth a thousand pieces of gold' ; ' As distance tests a horse's strength, so time reveals a person's heart' ; ' Humans die for money as birds die for food' ; ' Those who obey the will of heaven shall live; those who oppose it shall die' ; ' Honest advice may sound unpleasant but it induces good conduct; good medicine tastes bitter but it helps to cure disease' .

不 求 金 玉 重 重 贵
bù qiú jīn yù chóng chóng guì
但 愿 儿 孙 个 个 贤
dàn yuàn ér sūn gè gè xián

Crave not for money and valuables;
pray only that all your posterity will be morally upright.

1

不 因 渔 夫 引
bù　yīn　yú　fū　yǐn
怎 得 见 波 涛
zěn　dé　jiàn　bō　tāo

**If there were no fishermen to guide us,
how could we ever see the great waves of the ocean?**

差 之 毫 厘
chà zhī háo lí
失 之 千 里
shī zhī qiān lǐ

A miss is as good as a mile.

长 江 后 浪 推 前 浪

cháng jiāng hòu làng tuī qián làng

世 上 新 人 赶 旧 人

shì shàng xīn rén gǎn jiù rén

As in the Yangtze River the waves behind propel those in front, so in the human world each new generation does better than the old.

常 将 有 日 思 无 日
cháng jiāng yǒu rì sī wú rì
莫 把 无 时 当 有 时
mò bǎ wú shí dàn yǒu shí

**Be prepared for hard times when your days are good;
do not wait till times are hard and sigh for the good days.**

池　塘　积　水　为　防　旱
chí　táng　jī　shuǐ　wèi　fáng　hàn

田　地　深　耕　足　养　家
tián　dì　shēn　gēng　zú　yǎng　jiā

Store water in ponds to prevent drought;
plough the field deeply to grow enough food for the family.

触 来 莫 与 竞
chù lái mò yǔ jìng
事 过 心 头 凉
shì guò xīn tóu liáng

**When someone offends you, don't argue with him;
let the thing blow over, and all will be peaceful again.**

从 俭 入 奢 易
cóng jiǎn rù shē yì
从 奢 入 俭 难
cóng shē rù jiǎn nán

**It is easy for the frugal to become extravagant,
but hard for the lavish to be thrifty.**

但 将 冷 眼 看 螃 蟹
dàn jiāng lěng yǎn kàn páng xiè
看 你 横 行 到 几 时
kàn nǐ héng xíng dào jǐ shí
**Keep a clear eye on the crab (wicked person)
and see how long it can run amuck.**

当 时 若 不 登 高 望
dāng shí ruò bù dēng gāo wàng
谁 信 东 流 海 洋 深
shuí xìn dōng liú hǎi yáng shēn

**If you do not climb high to get a distant view,
how can you appreciate the magnificence of
the rivers flowing eastward into the sea?**

道 路 各 別
dào   lù   gè   bié
养 家 一 般
yǎng jiā yì bān

**There are different roads in life,
but the way to feed a family is generally the same.**

道　吾　好　者　是　吾　賊
dào　wú　hǎo　zhě　shì　wú　zéi
道　吾　恶　者　是　吾　师
dào　wú　è　zhě　shì　wú　shī

**The man who flatters me steals from me;
the man who tells me my faults is my teacher.**

得 宠 思 辱
dé chǒng sī rǔ
安 居 虑 危
ān jū lù wēi

**When in high favour, think of your days of disgrace;
in times of peace, be mindful of possible dangers.**

点 石 化 为 金
diǎn shí huà wéi jīn
人 心 犹 未 足
rén xīn yóu wèi zú

**Even if stones could be turned into gold by touching,
some men would still be discontented.**

读 书 须 用 意
dú　shū　xū　yòng　yì

一 字 值 千 金
yī　zì　zhí　qiān　jīn

**Study with a concentrated mind; one
word may be worth a thousand pieces of gold.**

15

儿 孙 自 有 儿 孙 福
ér sūn zì yǒu ér sūn fú
莫 为 儿 孙 做 牛 马
mò wèi ér sūn zuò niú mǎ

Children can take care of themselves when they grow up; parents need not overextend themselves for their sake.

凡　人　不　可　貌　相
fán　rén　bù　kě　mào　xiàng
海　水　不　可　斗　量
hǎi　shuǐ　bù　kě　dǒu　liáng

A man cannot be judged by his appearance,
nor the sea measured by a peck.

逢　人　且　说　三　分　话
féng rén qiě shuō sān fēn huà
未　可　全　抛　一　片　心
wèi kě quán pāo yī piàn xīn

Be slow to speak your mind;
always speak with caution and restraint.

富 从 升 合 起
fù　cóng　shēng　hé　qǐ
贫 因 不 算 来
pín　yīn　bú　suàn　lái

**Wealth begins with saving bit by bit;
poverty comes from misspending.**

夫 妻 相 合 好
fū qī xiāng hé hǎo

琴 瑟 与 笙 簧
qín sè yǔ shēng huáng

**Husband and wife who live happily together
are like musical instruments playing in harmony.**

富 人 思 来 年
fù　rén　sī　lái　nián
穷 人 思 眼 前
qióng　rén　sī　yǎn　qián

**The rich man thinks of the future,
the poor man cares only about the present.**

父 子 合 而 家 不 退
fù zǐ hé ér jiā bú tuì

兄 弟 合 而 家 不 分
xiōng dì hé ér jiā bù fēn

When father and sons live in harmony, the family will not decline; when brothers live in peace with each other, the family will not be broken up.

根 深 不 怕 风 摇 动
gēn shēn bú pà fēng yáo dòng
树 正 不 怕 月 影 斜
shù zhèng bú pà yuè yǐng xié

A tree with deep roots does not fear the swaying of the wind; one with a straight trunk does not mind if its shadow is cast aslant by the moon.

23

公 道 世 间 惟 白 发
gōng dào shì jiān wéi bái fà
贵 人 头 上 不 曾 饶
guì rén tóu shàng bù céng ráo

**Age is the world's one impartial law;
even the noblest are not spared.**

观 今 宜 鉴 古
guān jīn yí jiàn gǔ

无 古 不 成 今
wú gǔ bù chéng jīn

**Use the past as a mirror when studying the present;
there can be no present without the past.**

官 清 司 吏 瘦
guān qīng sī lì shòu

神 灵 庙 祝 肥
shén líng miào zhù féi

**When an official is honest, his clerks stay thin;
when the bodhisattva in a temple is benevolent,
the priests there grow fat.**

官 有 正 条
guān yǒu zhèng tiáo

民 有 私 约
mín yǒu sī yuē

**Officials have their codes of conduct;
and the common people, their personal obligations.**

国 乱 思 良 将
guó luàn sī liáng jiàng
家 贫 思 贤 妻
jiā pín sī xián qī

An emperor thinks of a good general when his country is in danger. A man misses his virtuous wife when he is in poverty.

合 理 可 作
hé　　lǐ　　kě　　zuò
小 利 莫 争
xiǎo　　lì　　mò　　zhēng

Do what is right, don't haggle over minor benefits.

黄　河　尚　有　澄　清　日
huáng hé shàng yǒu chéng qīng rì
岂　可　人　无　得　运　时
qǐ kě rén wú dé yùn shí

**Even the Yellow River may become clear someday;
how can a man's lot never improve?**

黄 金 未 为 贵
huáng jīn wèi wéi guì

安 乐 值 多 少
ān lè zhí duō shǎo

**Gold is not the most precious;
happiness is worth much more.**

会 使 不 在 家 豪 富
huì shǐ bú zài jiā háo fù
风 流 不 用 着 衣 多
fēng liú bú yòng zhuó yī duō

**One who spends money wisely need not be rich;
one who looks smart and attractive need not wear
fine clothes. (Fine feathers don't make fine birds.)**

记	得	少	年	骑	竹	马
jì	dé	shào	nián	qí	zhú	mǎ

看	看	又	是	白	头	翁
kàn	kàn	yòu	shì	bái	tóu	wēng

**Remember we used to ride bamboo horses in our childhood;
and now we are old men with grey hair. (Time flies.)**

既 坠 釜 甄
jì zhuì fǔ zhēn

反 顾 无 益
fǎn gù wú yì

Since the pot is already broken, what is the use of regretting?
(Do not cry over spilt milk.)

假 缎 染 就 真 红 色
jiǎ duàn rǎn jiù zhēn hóng sè

也 被 旁 人 说 是 非
yě bèi páng rén shuō shì fēi

Even when what you do is both good and right, there are people who will spread lies about it.

见 者 易
jiàn zhě yì

学 者 难
xué zhě nán

**Watching others do something is easy;
learning to do it yourself is hard.**

将 相 顶 头 堪 走 马
jiàng xiàng dǐng tóu kān zǒu mǎ

公 侯 肚 里 好 撑 船
gōng hóu dù lǐ hǎo chēng chuán

**The mind of a minister is as broad as a race course;
the stomach of a marquis is big enough to hold a boat.**

近 水 知 鱼 性
jìn shuǐ zhī yú xìng
近 山 识 鸟 音
jìn shān shí niǎo yīn

**He who lives by the water knows the habits of fish;
he who lives near the hills can tell the calls of birds.**

救人一命
jiù rén yī mìng
胜造七级浮屠
shèng zào qī jí fú tú

**Saving a person's life is better than
building a seven-storey Buddhist pagoda.**

惧 法 朝 朝 乐
jù   fǎ   zhāo   zhāo   lè

欺 公 日 日 忧
qī   gōng   rì   rì   yōu

**Obey the law and you're always happy;
cheat and you'll never be at ease.**

君子爱财
jūn zǐ ài cái
取之有道
qǔ zhī yǒu dào

**Gentlemen love wealth,
but they obtain it by honest means.**

口 说 不 如 身 逢
kǒu shuō bù rú shēn féng
耳 闻 不 如 目 见
ěr wén bù rú mù jiàn

To experience is better than to be told; seeing for oneself is better than hearing from others. (Seeing is believing.)

枯　木　逢　春　犹　再　发
kū　mù　féng　chūn　yóu　zài　fā
人　无　两　度　再　少　年
rén　wú　liǎng　dù　zài　shào　nián

A withered tree may sprout again in the spring,
but an old man can never become young again.

Dad, let's go out for a walk.

Dad, look at that withered tree. It's sprouting again.

A withered tree may sprout again in the spring, but an old man can never become young again.

礼 仪 生 于 富 足
lǐ yì shēng yú fù zú
盗 贼 出 于 贫 穷
dào zéi chū yú pín qióng

**Etiquette is born of opulence;
poverty breeds thieves.**

44

留 得 五 湖 明 月 在
liú dé wǔ hú míng yuè zài
不 愁 无 处 下 金 钩
bù chóu wú chù xià jīn gōu

So long as there's a clear lake, there's a place to fish.
(When there's life, there's hope.)

路 逢 险 处 须 当 避
lù féng xiǎn chù xū dāng bì

不 是 才 人 不 献 诗
bú shì cái rén bú xiàn shī

**Avoid dangers that you meet on the road;
recite not poetry to those who are not learned.**

路 遥 知 马 力
lù yáo zhī mǎ lì
事 久 知 人 心
shì jiǔ jiàn rén xīn

**A long road tests a horse's strength
and a long task proves a person's heart.**

灭 却 心 头 火
miè què xīn tóu huǒ
剔 起 佛 前 灯
tī qǐ fó qián dēng

**Quench the fire in your heart;
light the candle before the Buddha.**

Zhang San is such a bully! I'll beat the hell out of him.

Goodness! Li Si and Zhang San had a bloody fight, and both have been arrested.

Young people should learn to give in a little. Step back and you'll have lots of room to manoeuvre. Quench the fire in your heart and light the candle before the Buddha.

明 知 山 有 虎
míng zhī shān yǒu hǔ
莫 向 虎 山 行
mò xiàng hǔ shān xíng

**Don't go into the mountains
when you know there are tigers there.**

49

莫 笑 他 人 老
mò xiào tā rén lǎo
终 须 还 到 老
zhōng xū huán dào lǎo

Do not laugh at others who are old,
for you yourself will become old some day.

牡　丹　花　好　空　入　目
mǔ　dān　huā　hǎo　kōng　rù　mù
枣　花　虽　小　结　实　成
zǎo　huā　suī　xiǎo　jié　shí　chéng

**Peony flowers are nice to look at,
but date blossoms though small bear fruit.**

你 急 他 未 急
nǐ　jí　tā　wèi　jí

人 闲 心 不 闲
rén　xián　xīn　bù　xián

You may be in a hurry, but he is not.
The body may be resting, but the mind is not.

年 年 防 饥
nián nián fáng jī
夜 夜 防 盗
yè yè fáng dào

**Be prepared against famines every year;
guard against theft every night.**

宁 可 正 而 不 足
níng kě zhèng ér bù zú
不 可 邪 而 有 余
bù kě xié ér yǒu yú

**Better be an honest man of slender
means than reap profits dishonestly.**

54

贫 居 闹 市 无 人 识
pín jū nào shì wú rén shí
富 在 深 山 有 远 亲
fù zài shēn shān yǒu yuǎn qīn

When you are poor, no one shows interest in you even if you live on a busy street; when you are rich, distant relatives will come even if you dwell in the depth of a mountain.

贫 困 自 在
pín kùn zì zài
富 贵 多 忧
fù guì duō yōu

The poor are free from trammels;
the rich have much to worry about.

平　生　莫　作　皱　眉　事
píng shēng mò zuò zhòu méi shì

世　上　应　无　切　齿　人
shì shàng yīng wú qiè chǐ rén

**If a man never does anything to make others knit their brows,
no one in the world will ever gnash his teeth at him.**

平 生 只 会 量 人 短
píng shēng zhǐ huì liáng rén duǎn
何 不 回 头 把 自 量
hé bù huí tóu bǎ zì liáng

**For those who always see the faults of others,
why don't they look at themselves?**

钱 财 如 粪 土
qián cái rú fèn tǔ

仁 义 值 千 金
rén yì zhí qiān jīn

Money is a mere mass of muck;
kindness is worth a thousand pieces of gold.

千 经 万 典
qiān jīng wàn diǎn
孝 义 为 先
xiào yì wéi xiān

Of all codes and classics, filial piety comes first.

千 里 送 鹅 毛
qiān   lǐ   sòng   é   máo

寄 物 不 可 失
jì   wù   bù   kě   shī

A goose feather sent from afar may be a small gift,
but do not take it lightly for the love it brings is profound.

强中自有强中手

qiáng zhōng zì yǒu qiáng zhōng shǒu

恶人须用恶人磨

è rén xū yòng è rén mó

**However strong you are, there's always someone stronger;
a bully must be subdued by a greater bully.**

晴 干 不 肯 去
qíng gān bù kěn qù
直 待 雨 淋 头
zhí dài yǔ lín tóu

**Unwilling to go when it is clear and dry, they
procrastinate until it rains. (Make hay while the sun shines.)**

去　时　终　须　去
qù　shí　zhōng　xū　qù
再　三　留　不　住
zài　sān　liú　bú　zhù

You cannot keep something that must go.

饶 人 不 是 痴 汉
ráo rén bú shì chī hàn
痴 汉 不 会 饶 人
chī hàn bú huì ráo rén

**Those who forgive others are no fools;
only fools never forgive.**

忍 得 一 时 气
rěn dé yī shí qì
免 得 百 日 忧
miǎn dé bǎi rì yōu

**Keep your temper for the present
and avoid lots of trouble in the future.**

人 各 有 心
rén gè yǒu xīn

心 各 有 见
xīn gè yǒu jiàn

Everyone has his own ideas and views.

人 老 心 未 老
rén lǎo xīn wèi lǎo

人 穷 志 未 穷
rén qióng zhì wèi qióng

**Old in age but young in spirit;
poor but with high aspirations.**

Lord Zhang, may I borrow a *dou** of rice from you? I'll return it tomorrow.

You poor wretch, give me three good kowtows.

Lord Zhang, you are wrong. A man may be poor, but he has high aspirations.

68

*dou, a unit of dry measure for grain (= 1 decalitre)

人　情　莫　道　春　光　好
rén　qíng　mò　dào　chūn　guāng　hǎo
只　怕　秋　来　有　冷　时
zhǐ　pà　qiū　lái　yǒu　lěng　shí

**Do not say that human feelings are as
warm as the sunlight in spring; they may
turn cold with the wind and rain in autumn.**

人 情 似 水 分 高 下
rén qíng sì shuǐ fēn gāo xià

世 事 如 云 任 卷 舒
shì shì rú yún rèn juǎn shū

Human feelings are like water, they can tell what's high or low. World affairs are like clouds, forever changing.

人 生 知 足 何 时 足
rén shēng zhī zú hé shí zú

人 老 偷 闲 且 自 闲
rén lǎo tōu xián qiě zì xián

**A man will never feel contented all his life,
but when he's old and has the time he should ease up a bit.**

Uncle, you seem to be free today. Taking a walk?

A man will never feel contented all his life, but when he's old and has the time he should ease up a bit.

人　为　财　死
rén　wèi　cái　sǐ

鸟　为　食　亡
niǎo　wèi　shí　wáng

Humans die for money, as birds die for food.

人 无 千 日 好
rén wú qiān rì hǎo
花 无 百 日 红
huā wú bǎi rì hóng

No man is always lucky; no flower blooms forever.

人 无 远 虑
rén wú yuǎn lǜ
必 有 近 忧
bì yǒu jìn yōu

**He who doesn't have a long-range plan
will surely find trouble in the short run.**

Buy some more delicacies tomorrow.

My lord, we should save a little; we mustn't be so extravagant.

My lady, we've got more than enough for our next life, why save?

But, my lord, he who doesn't have a long-range plan will surely find trouble in the short run.

入 门 休 问 荣 枯 事
rù mén xiū wèn róng kū shì
观 看 容 颜 便 得 知
guān kàn róng yán biàn dé zhī

When you enter somebody's house, you needn't ask him how he's doing; his looks will tell you.

75

若　登　高　必　自　卑
ruò　dēng　gāo　bì　zì　bēi
若　涉　远　必　自　迩
ruò　shè　yuǎn　bì　zì　ěr

If a man climbs up a high mountain, he will inevitably feel small. If he makes a long journey, he will know what distance means.

若 争 小 可
ruò zhēng xiǎo kě

便 失 大 道
biàn shī dà dào

If you go for little things, you may lose big ones.
(Penny-wise, pound-foolish.)

杀 人 可 恕
shā rén kě shù
情 理 难 容
qíng lǐ nán róng

**A man may be pardoned for killing another, but
neither conscience nor reason will ever forgive him.**

少 小 不 努 力
shào xiǎo bù nǔ lì
老 大 徒 伤 悲
lǎo dà tú shāng bēi

**If you neglect to study when you are young,
you'll regret it when you grow up.
(Present neglect makes future regret.)**

使　口　不　如　自　走
shǐ　kǒu　bù　rú　zì　zǒu
求　人　不　如　求　己
qiú　rén　bù　rú　qiú　jǐ

To do is better than to send; to do it yourself is better than to ask others.

Old man, send for our son-in-law tomorrow to install curtains for this window.

Are you going to do it yourself?

It's not convenient for him; he lives so far away.

Yes, to do is better than to send; to do it yourself is better than to ask others.

爽 口 食 多 偏 作 病
shuǎng kǒu shí duō piān zuò bìng

快 心 事 过 恐 生 殃
kuài xīn shì guò kǒng shēng yāng

Too much good food brings on indigestion;
too much excitement may cause disaster.

A toast to your promotion.

Thanks.

I've been promoted.

How nice!

Master, what's happened?

谁　人　背　后　无　人　说
shuí　rén　bèi　hòu　wú　rén　shuō
那　个　人　前　不　说　人
nǎ　gè　rén　qián　bù　shuō　rén

Who has never been talked about behind his back?
Who has never talked about others?

生 死 由 命
shēng sǐ yóu mìng
富 贵 在 天
fù guì zài tiān

**Life and death are decreed by fate,
riches and honour are determined by Heaven.**

Your Majesty,
my father, tomorrow
I'll summon the
best doctors in
the country to
cure your
disease.

The disease has spread
to the vital organs. It's
beyond cure.

Your Majesty,
how could you
leave me?

万 事 劝 人 休 瞒 昧
wàn shì quàn rén xiū mán mèi
举 头 三 尺 有 神 灵
jǔ tóu sān chǐ yǒu shén líng

**Never do anything that offends your conscience;
there are gods just above who oversee everything.**

为 善 最 乐
wéi　shàn　zuì　lè
为 恶 难 逃
wéi　è　nán　táo

**Virtue is the greatest happiness;
vice will not go unpunished.**

Granny, here's some water.

My grandchildren, have a drink.

Mum, we've fetched some water for Granny.

Virtue is the greatest happiness; vice will not go unpunished.

屋 漏 更 遭 连 夜 雨
wū lòu gèng zāo lián yè yǔ
行 船 又 遇 顶 头 风
xíng chuán yòu yù dǐng tóu fēng

Misfortunes never come singly.

无 求 到 处 人 情 好
wú qiú dào chù rén qíng hǎo
不 饮 从 他 酒 价 高
bù yǐn cóng tā jiǔ jià gāo

When you don't ask favours, people like you better.
When you don't drink liquor, you won't mind the cost.

无 限 朱 门 生 饿 殍
wú xiàn zhū mén shēng è piǎo

几 多 白 屋 出 公 卿
jǐ duō bái wū chū gōng qīng

**Many who were born in wealthy homes starve to death,
and many born of poor families become great men.**

贤 妇 令 夫 贵
xián fù lìng fū guì

恶 妇 令 夫 败
è fù lìng fū bài

**An understanding wife helps her husband to prosper;
a wicked wife will only make her husband degenerate.**

闲 时 不 烧 香
xián shí bù shāo xiāng
急 时 抱 佛 脚
jí shí bào fó jiǎo

One who does not burn incense at normal times will have to embrace the Buddha's feet and pray for help in times of emergency.

相 见 易 得 好
xiāng jiàn yì dé hǎo

久 住 难 为 人
jiǔ zhù nán wéi rén

**It's easy to be friendly with someone you meet occasionally,
but difficult when you live together for a long time.**

相 论 逞 英 雄
xiāng lùn chěng yīng xióng

家 计 渐 渐 退
jiā jì jiàn jiàn tuì

A family will gradually go to the dogs if its members keep bragging about themselves.

Father, I worked the hardest in building this house, so I should get a larger part of it.

Father, we won our last lawsuit only because I wrote an excellent plaint, so I should get a larger share.

A family will gradually go to the dogs if its members keep bragging about themselves. How can this house stand after my death if you are so divided?

衙 门 八 字 开
yá mén bā zì kāi
有 理 无 钱 莫 进 来
yǒu lǐ wú qián mò jìn lái

**The Yamen (courthouse in old China) gate is open wide;
with right but no money, don't go inside.**

养 儿 防 老
yǎng　ér　fáng　lǎo
积 谷 防 饥
jī　gǔ　fáng　jī

Children are for one's old age as corn is for a famine.

养 军 千 日
yǎng jūn qiān rì

用 在 一 朝
yòng zài yì zhāo

**Training troops for a thousand days
is to use them at a moment's notice.**

药　能　医　假　病
yào　néng　yī　jiǎ　bìng
酒　不　解　真　愁
jiǔ　bù　jiě　zhēn　chóu

**Medicine can tell a fake illness,
but wine cannot cure a real worry.**

因 风 吹 火
yīn fēng chuī huǒ
用 力 不 多
yòng lì bù duō

It takes little effort to fan a fire with the wind.

英 雄 行 险 道
yīng xióng xíng xiǎn dào

富 贵 似 花 枝
fù guì sì huā zhī

**A hero must stand up to all tests;
wealth is like flowers that do not last.**

有 茶 有 酒 多 兄 弟
yǒu chá yǒu jiǔ duō xiōng dì
急 难 何 曾 见 一 人
jí nán hé céng jiàn yì rén

**When you are rich, you have many friends;
but when you are in danger, where are your friends?**

欲 求 生 富 贵
yù qiú shēng fù guì

须 下 死 工 夫
xū xià sǐ gōng fú

**To gain a high position and great wealth,
one must make great efforts. (No trials, no triumph.)**

远 水 难 救 近 火
yuǎn shuǐ nán jiù jìn huǒ
远 亲 不 如 近 邻
yuǎn qīn bù rú jìn lín

**Distant water cannot put out a fire nearby;
close neighbours are dearer than relatives far away.**

在 家 不 会 迎 宾 客
zài jiā bú huì yíng bīn kè

出 外 方 知 少 主 人
chū wài fāng zhī shǎo zhǔ rén

A man who is not hospitable to his guests at home will find few people hospitable to him when he is on the road. (Kindness is a two-way street.)

择 其 善 者 而 从 之
zé qí shàn zhě ér cóng zhī
其 不 善 者 而 改 之
qí bú shàn zhě ér gǎi zhī

Choose and follow what is good;
avoid and give up what is bad.

責 人 之 心 責 己
zé rén zhī xīn zé jǐ
恕 己 之 心 恕 人
shù jǐ zhī xīn shù rén

**Blame yourself as you would blame others;
forgive others as you would forgive yourself.**

乍 富 不 知 新 受 用
zhà fù bù zhī xīn shòu yòng
骤 贫 难 改 旧 家 风
zhòu pín nán gǎi jiù jiā fēng

Those who become rich overnight do not know how to enjoy their wealth; those who become poor suddenly find it hard to change their extravagant ways.

知 音 说 与 知 音 听
zhī yīn shuō yǔ zhī yīn tīng
不 是 知 音 莫 与 谈
bú shì zhī yīn mò yǔ tán

**Talk intimately to those who understand you,
not to those who do not.**

知 止 常 止
zhī zhǐ cháng zhǐ
终 身 不 耻
zhōng shēn bù chǐ

If a man knows when to stop, he'll never overstep the mark and he'll never be disgraced.

知 足 常 足
zhī zú cháng zú
终 身 不 辱
zhōng shēn bù rǔ

**The contented man is always happy;
he never feels disgraced.**

众 星 朗 朗
zhòng xīng lǎng lǎng

不 如 孤 月 独 明
bù rú gū yuè dú míng

**The light of a hundred stars is
not as bright as that of the moon.**

忠 言 逆 耳 利 于 行
zhōng yán nì ěr lì yú xíng
良 药 苦 口 利 于 病
liáng yào kǔ kǒu lì yú bìng

**Honest advice may sound unpleasant but
it induces good conduct; good medicine
tastes bitter but it helps to cure disease.**

You good-for-nothing! You didn't pay any attention to what the teacher was saying. Your composition is just plain rubbish.

My boy, my boy!

My boy, what your parents said are for your own good. Honest advice may sound unpleasant, but it induces good conduct; good medicine tastes bitter but it helps to cure disease.

自 恨 枝 无 叶
zì hèn zhī wú yè
莫 怨 太 阳 偏
mò yuàn tài yáng piān

A man should first see if he has made any mistakes himself; he should not always put the blame on others.

自　家　心　里　急
zì　jiā　xīn　lǐ　jí

他　人　未　知　忙
tā　rén　wèi　zhī　máng

Everyone has his own cares, which others never know.

Do you know these proverbs? Match the Chinese proverbs with the English translation below. Put the numerals 1-5 within the brackets.

1.　读　书　须　用　意
　　　　dú　shū　xū　yòng　yì
　　　一　字　值　千　金
　　　yī　zì　zhí　qiān　jīn

2.　少　小　不　努　力
　　　shào　xiǎo　bù　nǔ　lì
　　　老　大　徒　伤　悲
　　　lǎo　dà　tú　shāng　bēi

3.　闲　时　不　烧　香
　　　xián　shí　bù　shāo　xiāng
　　　急　时　抱　佛　脚
　　　jí　shí　bào　fó　jiǎo

4.　远　水　难　救　近　火
　　　yuǎn　shuǐ　nán　jiù　jìn　huǒ
　　　远　亲　不　如　近　邻
　　　yuǎn　qīn　bù　rú　jìn　lín

5.　路　遥　知　马　力
　　　lù　yáo　zhī　mǎ　lì
　　　事　久　知　人　心
　　　shì　jiǔ　jiàn　rén　xīn

Answers

(　　) One who does not burn incense at normal times will have to embrace the Buddha's feet and pray for help in times of emergency.

(　　) Study with a concentrated mind; one word may be worth a thousand pieces of gold.

(　　) A long road tests a horse's strength and a long task proves a person's heart.

(　　) If you neglect to study when you are young, you'll regret it when you grow up. (Present neglect makes future regret.)

(　　) Distant water cannot put out a fire nearby; close neighbours are dearer than relatives far away.

113

See page 115 for the answers. Answers for page 117: 25, 24, 21, 23, 22

Do you know these proverbs? Match the Chinese proverbs with the English translation below. Put the numerals 6-10 within the brackets.

6. 长 江 后 浪 推 前 浪
cháng jiāng hòu làng tuī qián làng

世 上 新 人 赶 旧 人
shì shàng xīn rén gǎn jiù rén

7. 凡 人 不 可 貌 相
fán rén bù kě mào xiàng

海 水 不 可 斗 量
hǎi shuǐ bù kě dǒu liáng

8. 口 说 不 如 身 逢
kǒu shuō bù rú shēn féng

耳 闻 不 如 目 见
ěr wén bù rú mù jiàn

9. 见 者 易
jiàn zhě yì

学 者 难
xué zhě nán

10. 千 里 送 鹅 毛
qiān lǐ sòng é máo

寄 物 不 可 失
jì wù bù kě shī

Answers ( ) **A man cannot be judged by his appearance, nor the sea measured by a peck.**

( ) **As in the Yangtze River the waves behind propel those in front, so in the human world each new generation does better than the old.**

( ) **A goose feather sent from afar may be a small gift, but do not take it lightly for the love it brings is profound.**

( ) **Watching others do something is easy; learning to do it yourself is hard.**

( ) **To experience is better than to be told; seeing for oneself is better than hearing from others. (Seeing is believing.)**

114

See page 116 for the answers. Answers for page 116: 19, 20, 16, 18, 17

Do you know these proverbs? Match the Chinese proverbs with the English translation below. Put the numerals 11-15 within the brackets.

11. 人 无 千 日 好
rén wú qiān rì hǎo
花 无 百 日 红
huā wú bǎi rì hóng

12. 为 善 最 乐
wéi shàn zuì lè
为 恶 难 逃
wéi è nán táo

13. 差 之 毫 厘
chà zhī háo lí
失 之 千 里
shī zhī qiān lǐ

14. 常 将 有 日 思 无 日
cháng jiāng yǒu rì sī wú rì
莫 把 无 时 当 有 时
mò bǎ wú shí dàn yǒu shí

15. 父 子 合 而 家 不 退
fù zǐ hé ér jiā bú tuì
兄 弟 合 而 家 不 分
xiōng dì hé ér jiā bù fēn

Answers

( ) A miss is as good as a mile.

( ) When father and sons live in harmony, the family will not decline; when brothers live in peace with each other, the family will not be broken up.

( ) Be prepared for hard times when your days are good; do not wait till times are hard and sigh for the good days.

( ) No man is always lucky; no flower blooms forever.

( ) Virtue is the greatest happiness; vice will not go unpunished.

See page 117 for the answers. Answers for page 113: 3, 1, 5, 2, 4

Do you know these proverbs? Match the Chinese proverbs with the English translation below. Put the numerals 16-20 within the brackets.

16. 明 知 山 有 虎
míng zhī shān yǒu hǔ

莫 向 虎 山 行
mò xiàng hǔ shān xíng

17. 强 中 自 有 强 中 手
qiáng zhōng zì yǒu qiáng zhōng shǒu

恶 人 须 用 恶 人 磨
è rén xū yòng è rén mó

18. 人 为 财 死
rén wèi cái sǐ

鸟 为 食 亡
niǎo wèi shí wáng

19. 因 风 吹 火
yīn fēng chuī huǒ

用 力 不 多
yòng lì bù duō

20. 忠 言 逆 耳 利 于 行
zhōng yán nì ěr lì yú xíng

良 药 苦 口 利 于 病
liáng yào kǔ kǒu lì yú bìng

Answers ( ) It takes little effort to fan a fire with the wind.

( ) Honest advice may sound unpleasant but it induces good conduct; good medicine tastes bitter but it helps to cure disease.

( ) Don't go into the mountains when you know there are tigers there.

( ) Humans die for money, as birds die for food.

( ) However strong you are, there's always someone stronger; a bully must be subdued by a greater bully.

See page 114 for the answers. Answers for page 114: 7, 6, 10, 9, 8

Do you know these proverbs? Match the Chinese proverbs with the English translation below. Put the numerals 21-25 within the brackets.

21. 千 经 万 典
qiān　jīng　wàn　diǎn

孝 义 为 先
xiào　yì　wéi　xiān

22. 君 子 爱 财
jūn　zǐ　ài　cái

取 之 有 道
qǔ　zhī　yǒu　dào

23. 莫 笑 他 人 老
mò　xiào　tā　rén　lǎo

终 须 还 到 老
zhōng　xū　huán　dào　lǎo

24. 人 老 心 未 老
rén　lǎo　xīn　wèi　lǎo

人 穷 志 未 穷
rén　qióng　zhì　wèi　qióng

25. 使 口 不 如 自 走
shǐ　kǒu　bù　rú　zì　zǒu

求 人 不 如 求 己
qiú　rén　bù　rú　qiú　jǐ

⸺⸺⸺⸺⸺⸺⸺⸺⸺⸺⸺⸺⸺⸺⸺⸺⸺⸺⸺⸺

Answers ( ) To do is better than to send; to do it yourself is better than to ask others.

( ) Old in age but young in spirit; poor but with high aspirations.

( ) Of all codes and classics, filial piety comes first.

( ) Do not laugh at others who are old, for you yourself will become old some day.

( ) Gentlemen love wealth, but they obtain it by honest means.

See page 113 for the answers. Answers for page 115: 13, 15, 14, 11, 12

GATEWAY TO CHINESE CLASSICAL LITERATURE

Chinese classical literature encompasses a dazzling range, from poetry, rhymed prose, essays to drama and novels. Despite the passage of time, these works remain fresh and relevant today. Using illustrations and lucid exposition of the various styles of classical Chinese literature, this book takes the reader on a tour of the Chinese literary world, at the same time affording valuable insights into the themes and social issues of early Chinese civilisation.

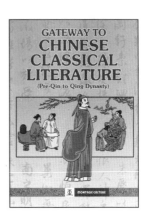

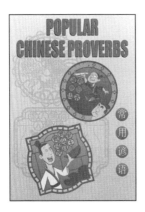

POPULAR CHINESE PROVERBS

Popular Chinese Proverbs collects several old favourites and some of the most widely used expressions. Using vibrant illustrations and clear explanations of the metaphors and history behind them, their origins and meanings are presented in an easy-to-understand format.

THE ART OF PEACE: PRACTICAL TEACHINGS OF MO ZI

During the chaotic Warring States Period (475 – 221 BC), when China was divided into numerous small states locked in endless conflict and power struggle, philosopher Mo Zi spread his message of peace and universal love.

VALUES FOR SUCCESS

STORIES OF LOYALTY
Illustrated by **Ren Changhong,** *210 x 150mm, 144pp, ISBN 981-229-083-4.*
Confucius says: "To all you serve, be loyal." Whether it is towards the country, people or friends, one should be always loyal.

STORIES OF FILIAL PIETY
Illustrated by **Tan Choon Wai,** *210 x 150mm, 144pp, ISBN 981-229-091-5.*
Contains accounts of people in ancient China known for their extraordinary devotion to their parents.

STORIES OF KINDNESS
Illustrated by **Huang Qingrong**, *210 x 150mm, 136pp, ISBN 981-229-098-2.*
Find out how the respect for life is expressed in acts of kindness.

STORIES OF LOVE
Illustrated by **Huang Qingrong**, *210 x 150mm,136pp, ISBN 981-229-099-0.*
Love inspires us to live each day to the fullest. It also nurtures the soul for when we love others, we make them feel significant.

STORIES OF PROPRIETY
Illustrated by **Ren Changhong,** *210 x 150mm, 136pp, ISBN 981-229-094-X.*
Important historical figures such as Zhou Gong and Liu Bei show us the importance of propriety.

STORIES OF RIGHTEOUSNESS
Illustrated by **Goh Ngoh Seng,** *210 x 150mm, 136pp, ISBN 981-229-095-8.*
Accounts of Chinese historical figures who did righteous deeds will rekindle in us the spirit of love and kindness.

STORIES OF INTEGRITY
Illustrated by **Huang Qingrong,** *210 x 150mm, 136pp, ISBN 981-229-096-6.*
Integrity is one of the virtues which make up the moral fabric of a society. You will be inspired by fine examples of integrity.

STORIES OF HONOUR
Illustrated by **Fu Chunjiang**, *210 x 150mm, 136pp, ISBN 981-229-097-4.*
Many historical personages have endured shame innocently and made a decisive comeback.

CHINESE CULTURE SERIES

150x210mm, fully illustrated

ORIGINS OF CHINESE PEOPLE AND CUSTOMS

Explores the beginnings of the Chinese people, origins of Chinese names, Chinese zodiac signs, the afterlife, social etiquette and more!

ORIGINS OF CHINESE FESTIVALS

Stories about Lunar New Year, Chinese Valentine's Day, Qing Ming, Dragon Boat, Zhong Yuan, Mid-Autumn Festivals and more.

ORIGINS OF CHINESE MUSIC AND ART

Interesting facts about the "Four Treasures of the Study": the brush, ink, paper and inkstone, which form the cornerstone of Chinese culture.

ORIGINS OF CHINESE FOLK ARTS

Packed with useful information on artistic interests covering Chinese embroidery, lacquerware, paper cutting, face masks and pottery.

ORIGINS OF CHINESE MARTIAL ARTS
Traces the origins of the *gongfu* of Shaolin and Wudang warriors and their philosophy and chivalry code.

ORIGINS OF CHINESE CUISINE
Showcases famous and best-relished dishes, including Peking Roast Duck and Buddha Jumps Over the Wall, and the stories behind them.

ORIGINS OF CHINESE FOOD CULTURE
Covers the origins, history, customs, and the art and science of Chinese food culture, including the 18 methods of cooking.

ORIGINS OF CHINESE TEA AND WINE
Explores the origins, history, customs, and the art of Chinese tea and wine, including stories of how famous varieties of tea and wine came to be.

ORIGINS OF CHINESE SCIENCE & TECHNOLOGY
Covers great inventions by the Chinese: the compass, paper-making, gunpowder and printing. Also explores Chinese expertise in the fields of geography, mathematics, agriculture and astronomy.

增 广 贤 文

编著 ：陈望衡、李小香

绘画 ：徐丽廷、傅一纯

翻译 ：龚理曾、杨爱文

亚太图书有限公司出版